ustice and Fairness

by Isaac Seder

RAINTREE
STECK-VAUGHN
RSVP PUBLISHERS

A Harcourt Company

Austin   New York
www.raintreesteckvaughn.com

Published by Raintree Steck-Vaughn Publishers, an imprint of Steck-Vaughn Company.

Library of Congress Cataloging-in-Publication Data

Seder, Isaac.
    Fairness and justice / Isaac Seder.
        p. cm. — (Character education)
    Summary: Examines the related concepts of fairness and justice and explains their meaning of equal treatment for individuals, families, communities, and nations.
    Includes bibliographical references and index.
    ISBN 0-7398-5805-X
    1. Fairness—Juvenile literature. 2. Justice—Juvenile literature.
3. Conduct of life—Juvenile literature. [1. Fairness. 2. Justice. 3. Conduct of life.] I. Title. II. Character education (Raintree Steck-Vaughn Publishers)
BJ1533.F2 S44 2002
179'.9—dc21   2002017800

Printed and bound in China
1 2 3 4 5 6 7 8 9 10   05 04 03 02

A Creative Media Applications, Inc. Production

Photo Credits:
PhotoDisc:Cover
AP/Wide World Photographs: Pages 5, 6, 7, 9, 13, 14, 17, 19, 20, 21, 22, 23, 25, 27, 28, 29

Editor: Matt Levine
Indexer: Joan Verniero
Design and Production: Alan Barnett, Inc.
Photo Research: Yvette Reyes

Contents

"It is reasonable that everyone who asks justice should do justice."
—Thomas Jefferson, Third U.S. president and author of the Declaration of Independence

"That's not fair!"

You have probably heard that sentence at least a hundred times. But what does it mean when something is not fair? Compare these two examples.

- There are two slices of pizza. One is a bit smaller than the other. Maria grabs the larger piece and Koji loudly whines, "That's not fair!"

- Alison sees everyone playing kickball except Nate. Alison finds out that Nate asked to play, but the others would not let him. "That's not fair," says Alison. "Let's do something about it."

Getting your fair share is okay, but fairness is much more than getting equal slices of pizza.

Hannah Gargasz, 10, left, and Alyssa Rodriguez, 9, cheer during a game of kickball at St. Marys School, in Vermilion, Ohio. What would you do if you saw some kids who would not let a new student join their kickball game?

Both of these examples are about fairness, but only one deals with the big issue. When Koji complains about the pizza, he is more interested in himself than fairness. Being fair is a lot more than just getting enough pizza. Alison's actions show that she understands the big idea behind fairness. It is not fair to keep Nate from playing.

Being fair means following the rules and acting in a way that gives everyone an equal opportunity, or chance. Fairness is an important **value** that reflects your respect for others and your concern for equality. The ideas in this book will help you think about your own sense of fairness.

How Rules Hold Things Together

Being fair means playing by the rules. When you play a game, fair play means that everyone follows the same rules.

Playing fair is not just a noble idea—it actually makes playing games possible! Imagine what would happen if baseball players made up their own rules. The pitcher might decide to use a golf ball instead

How does an umpire help players stick to the rules?

of a baseball so that batters would have more trouble hitting the ball. Then a batter might pick up a tennis racket instead of a bat. Soon the game would fall apart.

Rules make sure that everyone is playing the same game in the same way. Rules do not favor one side or the other. They give both sides an equal chance to win. You cannot follow the rules unless you know what they are. When you play any game, make sure that you know the rules.

If you are playing a game with friends, you can make up your own rules, too. Just make sure that everyone knows the rules *before* you begin playing. That way everyone plays by the same rules. Talk over the rules for just a minute or two before you start. Your game will be more fair—and more fun—that way.

Rules and fair play are not just for sports. Your family might have rules about anything from chores and homework to snacks and watching television. These rules hold your family together in the same way that rules hold a baseball game together. Your **community** also has rules, or **laws.** Laws are the rules that everyone in a community agrees to follow. They help make sure that everyone is treated equally.

Signs in your school may list rules to follow.
How else can you find out about school rules?

Adam can never remember how to spell *tomorrow*. Right before a spelling quiz, he writes the word on his hand so that he will get it right.

Adam is cheating. He is breaking the quiz rules. He might get a point for spelling the word correctly, but he will not have earned it. When he washes his hand, he still will not know how to spell *tomorrow*. Adam's cheating hurts himself. He does not learn what he is supposed to learn.

Is It Cheating?

It can be hard to tell if someone is cheating. You be the judge for these cases.

- Max has to take a test that his older brother already took. He decides to ask his brother what the test is like.

- Leona starts running a second before a race actually begins. No one catches her starting early.

- A school dog show only allows dogs more than six months old. Hani does not know the rule and enters her five-month-old puppy.

What is wrong with cheating on a test? Think about why you have to take tests. It is to see if you have learned something.

Other people can be hurt when someone cheats, too. Naomi enters a kids' poetry contest. Her aunt helps to write her poem, even though the rules say that no adult help is allowed. If Naomi wins, the contest is not fair to anyone else who has entered it. By asking her aunt for help, she has not followed the rules of the contest.

Cheating is never fair. No matter how tempting it might be to take the easy road, cheating is always a bad choice.

Making Fair Decisions

The decisions that you make reflect your own sense of what is fair. If you are a fair person, you will always take the time to make decisions that treat everyone equally. Think about what can happen if you rush a decision.

Lily is judging an essay contest for her school newspaper. However, she does not have time to read all the essays. She decides to pick a winner from those essays

If you had to decide between inviting two friends to a birthday party, how could you make a fair decision?

Decision-Making Action Plan

Follow the plan here to help you make fair decisions.

- Clearly understand exactly what you must decide. Make sure that you understand how your decision will affect everyone.

- Get all the information you need. You can find information by reading at the library, searching the Internet, or asking friends and experts.

- Make a list of every possible choice.

- Compare your choices. Why is each choice better or worse than the others?

- Make a decision. Try explaining to a friend why your decision is best. If you cannot explain your choice clearly, you may want to think more about it.

that she has already read.

This decision is unfair to everyone. The kids who entered the contest deserve to have their work read. The people who read the newspaper deserve to read the best essay.

Lily may feel like she has no other choice, but she is not thinking hard enough. She can ask for help reading the entries. She also might be able to extend the contest deadline.

Raul is from Mexico. His adopted brother is Chinese. Some of Raul's Mexican neighbors never speak to his brother because they think that he is not interested in their community.

Greg, Alana, and John are the student editors of a school poetry magazine. They promise their friends that they will publish their poems even before they have read them.

Both of these situations are unfair. They are examples of **prejudice.** Prejudice means making a judgment before

Getting to Know People

These tips will help you meet new people without being prejudiced.

- Focus on the ways in which you are alike. Find things that you have in common.

- Respect your differences. No one's way is better than yours and yours is not better than anyone else's. Different does not have to mean better or worse.

- Treat others the way that you want to be treated.

Joseph Allen waves the American flag as civil rights activist Dr. Johnnie Carr leads the singing of "We Shall Overcome" on the steps of the Alabama state capitol. Many people have fought to gain equal rights for all citizens in the United States.

all of the facts are known. Prejudice can also mean judging someone based on how he or she looks.

Raul's Mexican neighbors are prejudiced against his adopted Chinese brother even though they have never met him. Some people may be prejudiced against certain religions or against men or women.

The poetry editors are prejudiced in favor of their friends. This might sound okay, but it is still unfair. To be fair, the editors should make their decisions based on the quality of the poetry, not who wrote the poems.

Issues of fairness are bound to come up with the people that you know. In fact, they cannot be avoided. Fairness is not a math problem. Not everyone always gets exactly the same things at the same time. That is just not possible.

So it is important not to overreact when you think that something is unfair. If your brother gets to go to the movies and you have to stay home to finish your homework, do not squawk, "It's not fair!" Is this is a

Do you need to have a talk with your family?
You might start the discussion when everyone
is relaxed after a sharing a meal together.

Talking It Over

Do you need to talk about something that is just not fair? Use these hints to help you make your case.

- Stay calm. Try not to let anger get the better of you.

- Explain your feelings slowly and exactly.

- Watch the tone of your voice. Whining, shouting, or sounding angry will not help you make your point. Aim for a confident, reasonable tone.

- Listen carefully to the response that you get. Try not to react until you understand the other person's point of view.

seriously unfair situation? Your parents probably have pretty good reasons for treating the two of you differently.

Still there will be times when you think something is truly unfair. When you feel strongly about a fairness issue, you should not hesitate to talk about it. Your friends or family will never know how you feel unless they hear it from you.

When thinking about fairness in your family, it is important to remember that your parents have the final say. You need to respect their rules and decisions. If you disagree, use the tips on this page to help you make your point.

Being Fair to Yourself

There is one more person that you need to treat fairly—yourself. Think about how these two students are treating themselves.

Lenny eagerly signed up for guitar classes but usually does not practice between classes. He finds the classes frustrating because he is improving so slowly.

Sonja is involved in so many after-school activities that she does not have time to just read a book for fun. She really misses reading.

Both Lenny and Sonja are not treating themselves fairly. Lenny is not taking advantage of a great chance to learn to play the guitar. He must be interested, because he signed up for the classes. By not practicing, he is not getting much out of the experience. Sonja is cheating herself of one of her greatest pleasures because she has overbooked her time.

To treat yourself fairly, you need to take advantage of opportunities and then stick to your choices. Football coach George Allen said, "Each of us has been put on earth with the ability to do something well. We cheat ourselves and the world if we don't use that ability as best we can."

It may take you some time to find your strengths and abilities. When you start a new project, do not expect instant success. Give yourself time to learn, and you will be rewarded with new skills.

Every day is full of possibilities. How can you fairly balance the things that you have to do with the things that you want to do?

When people look at fairness from a community, state, or national viewpoint, they usually use another word to describe it. This word is justice, and it is a cornerstone of the U.S. government.

Justice is fair and right treatment under the law. Every **citizen** deserves to be treated fairly and equally by the law.

When a situation is not just, citizens can work together to make changes. United States history is filled with examples. Slavery is unjust and inhuman. Although it took time and hard work, citizens and leaders finally did

A Declaration and a Powerful Pledge

The idea of justice is powerful in the United States. It goes back to the Declaration of Independence, which was written by Thomas Jefferson in 1776. Students at most public schools show their support for the idea of justice every day when they say the Pledge of Allegiance:

I pledge allegiance to the flag of the United States of America and to the republic for which it stands, one nation, indivisible, with liberty and justice for all.

Susan B. Anthony, left, and Elizabeth Cady Stanton sit on the porch in Rochester, New York, in this undated photo. The two 19th-century women were deeply involved in gaining the vote for American women.

Dr. Martin Luther King, Jr., and other civil rights leaders fought for justice for black Americans. Here King acknowledges the crowd at the Lincoln Memorial for his "I Have a Dream" speech in Washington, D.C., on August 28, 1963.

away with slavery and brought justice to black Americans.

You can take action to improve justice in your community, state, or country. If you think a law or regulation is unjust, speak up. It is your job to do so as a member of this country. Write to politicians and other leaders to let them know how you feel. Work with other students and adults to make sure that everyone is treated fairly.

When dealing with crime, the justice system of the United States is special. It tries to ensure two things: Criminals will be punished, and the rights of **innocent** people will be protected.

A criminal trial in the United States uses some basic rules to get fair results. When a crime is committed, the police look for proof that can be used to find the

This is an artist's sketch of a Los Angeles, California, courtroom. All Americans have the right to a speedy trial.

Detective Richard Teesma of the New York Police bomb squad gathered clues at a crime scene and made this model. The model is being used in court to help determine if someone is guilty or innocent.

criminal. Once a suspect has been arrested, the police must tell the suspect about his or her rights. Suspects have several rights under the law. These rights are an attempt to make sure that the justice system is fair to the suspects.

For example, suspects have the right to have a lawyer, even if they cannot afford to pay for one. Suspects also have the right to a "speedy" trial. They must be tried in a reasonable amount of time after being arrested.

An arrest does not mean that a person is **guilty.** According to the American idea of fairness, any person is considered innocent of a crime until he or she has gone to trial and been found guilty. An arrest means only that there is "probable cause" to believe that the person has committed the crime.

A courtroom is filled with many people working together to make sure that a suspect gets a fair trial. Here are some of the people that you would be likely to see during a trial.

- The defendant is the person on trial for committing a crime.

- The defense attorney is the lawyer for the defendant. The defense attorney tries to prove the defendant is innocent.

A defendant, far left, sits with his lawyers.

- The prosecutor is the lawyer for the government. The prosecutor tries to prove the defendant is guilty.

- The judge is in charge of what happens in the courtroom. He or she makes sure that the trial is fair and legal.

A judge listens carefully to the details of a case to ensure that a fair trial takes place.

- The jury is a group of people who decide whether the defendant is innocent or guilty. The jury listens to the details presented during the trial and makes a decision based on the facts and the law.

- A witness is someone who has information to share about a trial. For example, a witness might have seen the crime or might know the defendant personally. The jury can learn a lot of information by listening carefully to every witness.

The U.S. justice system is known as "trial by jury." The American idea of trial by jury is a new one. The jury is a big part of what makes this justice system fair.

A jury is supposed to be made up of 12 citizens. After a trial, the jury goes to a separate room and discusses the facts of the trial. They try to reach a **verdict.** A verdict is the jury's decision about the guilt or innocence of the person accused. The jury's discussion can take hours or days, depending on the case. Juries must take their job very seriously because someone's future is at stake.

While the trial is taking place, members of the jury are

Beyond a Reasonable Doubt

In the United States, the law says that guilt must be proven "beyond a reasonable doubt." That means that the jury must be fully convinced. If the jury feels that there is any doubt about a suspect's guilt, it must decide that he or she is innocent. The rule of "beyond a reasonable doubt" makes sure that trials are as fair as possible.

Most juries have 12 people, but there are often two alternate jurors. If a juror gets sick or cannot continue, an alternate takes over.

not allowed to talk about it. They are also not supposed to read articles or watch television news about the trial. Reading or watching news outside the trial might prevent them from reaching a fair verdict.

In the United States, for a person to be found guilty, all 12 members of the jury must agree on the verdict. The jury must believe that the accused is guilty "beyond a reasonable doubt."

Some people believe that the American system gives too much protection to people who are accused of crimes. However, these protections show how much importance Americans place on the values of fairness and justice.

Thurgood Marshall: A Portrait of Justice

The word justice can be more than just an idea. It can refer to a person. *Justice* is another term for a courtroom judge. The U.S. Supreme Court is the highest court in the country. Supreme Court justices evaluate cases that deal with equality and fairness for the entire country. Few people have fought more for fairness and justice than Supreme Court Justice Thurgood Marshall.

Thurgood Marshall was the first black Supreme Court justice. He was a tireless fighter for civil rights.

Marshall grew up in Baltimore, Maryland. He went to an all-black public school. At that time in Maryland, black students and white students were not allowed to attend public school together. This is called **segregation.**

After graduating from Howard University, Marshall used his role as a lawyer to help make changes. He took part in many cases that focused on issues of racial equality, particularly on segregation.

Marshall's most famous case was *Brown v. Board of Education of Topeka, Kansas*. Marshall said that segregated public schools were against the laws of the Constitution. In 1954, the U.S. Supreme Court agreed with him. This was one of the most important rulings in U.S. history. It led to the end of segregation in all parts of public life.

In 1967 President Lyndon B. Johnson selected Marshall for the U.S. Supreme Court. This is the highest honor that a lawyer or judge can receive. Marshall served on the court until he retired in 1991.

George E.C. Hayes, left, Thurgood Marshall, center, and James M. Nabrit were the lawyers who led the fight before the U.S. Supreme Court that ended segregation in public schools on May 17, 1954.

"That's not fair!"

Those words should have a different meaning for you now. They are much more than just a way to get your fair share. They say that someone is being treated unequally.

Take a look at some of the world leaders on this page and the next. Each of them has made fairness a lifetime goal. You do not need to be a world leader to take fairness seriously. What can you do? Show that you value fairness by taking action whenever you find an unfair situation.

Make fairness a part of every day and every decision. Soon you will be turning the unhappy sound of "That's not fair!" into a joyous shout: "Now *that's* fair!"

Archbishop Desmond Tutu of South Africa talks to a crowd in Cleveland, Ohio, in 1999. Tutu is a civil rights leader who has won the Nobel Peace Prize.

Fairness Fighters

Many famous leaders have helped people around the world gain fair and just treatment.

- Mexican-American Cesar Chavez raised his voice against the unfair treatment of poor farm workers in California.

- In Burma, Nobel-prize winner Aung San Suu Kyi has challenged a brutal military dictatorship with calls for democracy. She has been honored with the Nobel Peace Prize for her work.

Cesar Chavez speaks at a Los Angeles, California, news conference on March 8, 1989.

Aung San Suu Kyi, pro-democracy leader of the National League for Democracy, at a 1996 press conference in Rangoon, Burma.

Glossary

Citizen: A member of a country, nation, city, or town

Community: A group of people who live, learn, or work in the same area

Guilty: Responsible for a crime or for wrong

Innocent: Not responsible for a crime or for wrong

Laws: The written rules that a society lives by.

Prejudice: Judgment of people without all the facts

Segregation: The practice of keeping groups separate

Values: Ideas that are important to people

Verdict: The jury's decision about the guilt or innocence of the person accused

Aldred, Lisa. *Thurgood Marshall (Black Americans of Achievement)*. Broomall, PA: Chelsea House, 1990.
This full-length biography of Thurgood Marshall provides an in-depth look at his lifelong fight for justice.

Taylor, Mildred D. *Roll of Thunder, Hear My Cry*. New York, NY: Dial, 1976.
This Newbery Medal-winning novel describes the unfairness and prejudice that nine-year-old Cassie Logan experiences as she grows up in the American South of the 1930s.

www.usdoj.gov/kidspage/
This web site, Justice for Kids and Youth, from the Department of Justice highlights a variety of topics related to justice.

Index